Table Of Contents

The Importance of Cyber Security Training 2
Overview of Different Types of Cyber Security Training 2
Chapter 2: Incident Response Training 2
    Understanding Incident Response 2
    Developing an Incident Response Plan 2
Chapter 3: Network Security Training 2
    Basics of Network Security 2
    Common Network Security Threats 2
Chapter 4: Cloud Security Training 2
    Securing Cloud Infrastructure 2
    Best Practices for Cloud Security 2
Chapter 5: Mobile Security Training 2

- Mobile Device Security 2
- Mobile App Security 2
- Chapter 6: Web Application Security Training 2
  - Common Web Application Vulnerabilities 2
  - Secure Coding Practices 2
- Chapter 7: Industrial Control System Security Training 2
  - Understanding Industrial Control Systems 2
  - Securing Industrial Control Systems 2
- Chapter 8: Cyber Threat Intelligence Training 2
  - Introduction to Cyber Threat Intelligence 2
  - Utilizing Threat Intelligence for Defense 2
- Chapter 9: Security Awareness Training for Employees 2
  - Importance of Security Awareness 2
  - Developing an Effective Security Awareness Program 2
- Chapter 10: Advanced Cyber Security Techniques 2
  - Penetration Testing 2
  - Incident Response Simulation Exercises 2
- Chapter 11: Ethical Hacking Training 2
  - Introduction to Ethical Hacking 2
  - Hands-on Hacking Exercises 2
- Chapter 12: Conclusion and Next Steps 2
  - Recap of Key Concepts 2
  - Continuing Education Opportunities 2
- Chapter 1: Introduction to Cyber Security Training 1

Chapter 1: Introduction to Cyber Security Training

The Importance of Cyber Security Training

In today's digital age, cyber security training has never been more important for corporate IT departments. With the constant threat of cyber attacks looming, it is crucial for organizations to invest in training programs that will help their employees defend against potential threats. Cyber security training not only helps in preventing attacks, but also equips IT professionals with the necessary skills to respond effectively in the event of a breach.

One of the key reasons why cyber security training is so important is because it helps IT departments stay ahead of constantly evolving cyber threats. By providing employees with up-to-date training on the latest cyber security trends and techniques, organizations can better protect their sensitive data and systems. This proactive approach to cyber security can help prevent costly data breaches and downtime, saving companies both time and money in the long run.

Incident response training is another crucial aspect of cyber security training that organizations should prioritize. In the event of a cyber attack, it is essential for IT professionals to know how to effectively respond and mitigate the damage. By investing in incident response training, organizations can ensure that their IT teams are well-prepared to handle any security incidents that may arise, minimizing the impact on the business.

Network security training is also essential for corporate IT departments, as networks are often the primary target for cyber attacks. By providing employees with training on how to secure their networks, organizations can prevent unauthorized access and protect their sensitive data. This training can include everything from setting up firewalls and VPNs to implementing strong password policies and monitoring network traffic for suspicious activity.

Overall, cyber security training is essential for all organizations, regardless of their size or industry. By investing in training programs that cover a wide range of topics, including incident response, network security, cloud security, and more, organizations can better protect their data and systems from cyber threats. With cyber attacks becoming increasingly sophisticated, it is more important than ever for IT departments to prioritize cyber security training and ensure that their employees have the knowledge and skills needed to defend against potential threats.

Overview of Different Types of Cyber Security Training

In the digital age, cyber security training has become essential for all organizations to protect their sensitive data and infrastructure from malicious cyber attacks. There are various types of cyber security training programs available to help corporate IT departments strengthen their defenses and respond effectively to cyber threats. This subchapter will provide an overview of the different types of cyber security training available, including incident response training, network security training, cloud security training, mobile security training, web application security training, industrial control system security training, cyber threat intelligence training, and security awareness training for employees.

Incident response training is crucial for organizations to effectively detect, respond to, and recover from cyber security incidents. This type of training prepares IT professionals to quickly assess the situation, contain the threat, and mitigate any damage caused by the attack. By simulating real-world cyber security incidents, employees can practice their response skills and ensure that they are well-prepared to handle any potential threats.

Network security training focuses on securing an organization's network infrastructure from unauthorized access and potential cyber attacks. This type of training covers topics such as network architecture, firewalls, intrusion detection systems, and secure communication protocols.

By understanding the fundamentals of network security, IT professionals can better protect their organization's data and systems from external threats.

Cloud security training is essential for organizations that store their data and applications in the cloud. This type of training covers topics such as data encryption, access control, and secure cloud configurations. By implementing best practices for cloud security, organizations can ensure that their data remains protected from unauthorized access and cyber attacks.

Mobile security training is designed to help IT professionals secure mobile devices and applications used within the organization. This type of training covers topics such as mobile device management, secure coding practices, and mobile security policies. By implementing effective mobile security measures, organizations can prevent data breaches and protect sensitive information stored on mobile devices.

Web application security training focuses on securing web applications from common vulnerabilities and cyber attacks. This type of training covers topics such as secure coding practices, web application firewalls, and penetration testing. By implementing robust security measures for web applications, organizations can prevent unauthorized access and protect their data from cyber threats.

Chapter 2: Incident Response Training

Understanding Incident Response

Understanding incident response is a crucial aspect of maintaining strong cybersecurity defenses within any organization. In today's digital age, the threat of cyber attacks is ever-present, making it essential for corporate IT departments to be prepared to respond effectively when incidents occur. Incident response refers to the process of detecting, analyzing, and responding to security incidents in order to minimize damage and prevent future attacks.

When it comes to incident response, speed is of the essence. The longer it takes to detect and respond to a security incident, the more damage can be done. This is why it is important for IT departments to have a well-defined incident response plan in place. This plan should outline the steps that need to be taken in the event of a security incident, including who is responsible for each task and how communication will be handled throughout the process.

One key aspect of incident response is containment. Once a security incident has been detected, it is essential to contain the damage as quickly as possible in order to prevent it from spreading further. This may involve isolating affected systems, shutting down compromised accounts, or blocking malicious traffic. By containing the incident, IT departments can limit the impact on the organization and prevent further damage from occurring.

Another important aspect of incident response is analysis. Once the incident has been contained, IT departments must analyze the incident to determine its cause, impact, and scope. This may involve conducting forensic analysis, reviewing log files, and interviewing personnel involved in the incident. By understanding how the incident occurred, IT departments can better prepare for future incidents and strengthen their cybersecurity defenses.

In conclusion, incident response is a critical component of cybersecurity that all organizations must prioritize. By understanding the importance of incident response and having a well-defined plan in place, corporate IT departments can effectively detect, analyze, and respond to security incidents in a timely manner. By investing in incident response training and ensuring that all personnel are prepared to handle security incidents, organizations can better protect themselves from cyber threats and minimize the impact of attacks.

Developing an Incident Response Plan

Developing an Incident Response Plan is a crucial step in ensuring the security of your organization's digital assets. In today's digital age, cyber attacks are becoming increasingly sophisticated and prevalent, making it essential for organizations to be prepared to respond effectively in the event of a security breach. This subchapter will provide guidance on how to develop an incident response plan that is tailored to your organization's specific needs and requirements.

The first step in developing an incident response plan is to conduct a thorough risk assessment to identify potential vulnerabilities and threats to your organization's digital infrastructure. This assessment should include an analysis of your organization's network, systems, applications, and data to determine where weaknesses may exist and how they can be exploited by malicious actors. By understanding your organization's unique risk profile, you can better prioritize your response efforts and allocate resources accordingly.

Once you have identified potential risks, the next step is to define roles and responsibilities within your incident response team. This team should include representatives from your IT department, HR department, and cyber security professionals, as well as external experts such as ethical hackers who can provide valuable insights into potential attack vectors. Each team member should have a clear understanding of their role in the incident response process and be trained on how to effectively respond to security incidents.

In addition to defining roles and responsibilities, it is important to establish communication protocols and escalation procedures that will enable your incident response team to respond quickly and efficiently in the event of a security breach. This may include establishing a secure communication channel for team members to share information, coordinating with external stakeholders such as law enforcement and regulatory agencies, and developing a clear chain of command for decision-making during a crisis.

Finally, it is essential to regularly test and update your incident response plan to ensure that it remains effective in the face of evolving cyber threats. This may involve conducting simulated cyber attack exercises, known as "red team" exercises, to test your team's response capabilities and identify areas for improvement. By continuously refining your incident response plan based on lessons learned from these exercises, you can better prepare your organization to defend against cyber attacks and mitigate the impact of security incidents.

Chapter 3: Network Security Training

Basics of Network Security

Network security is a critical aspect of protecting corporate IT systems from cyber threats. As technology continues to advance, so do the methods used by hackers to breach network defenses. It is essential for corporate IT departments to have a solid understanding of the basics of network security in order to effectively safeguard sensitive data and prevent cyber attacks.

One of the fundamental principles of network security is the concept of defense in depth. This approach involves implementing multiple layers of security measures to protect the network from various types of attacks. By using a combination of firewalls, intrusion detection systems, antivirus software, and encryption technologies, IT departments can create a strong defense that makes it more difficult for hackers to compromise the network.

Another important aspect of network security is the practice of regular security audits and assessments. By conducting routine scans of the network infrastructure, IT departments can identify potential vulnerabilities and weaknesses that could be exploited by cyber attackers. This allows them to take proactive measures to address these issues before they can be used to breach the network.

In addition to implementing technical security measures, it is also crucial for corporate IT departments to educate employees about best practices for network security. This includes training them on how to create secure passwords, recognize phishing scams, and avoid downloading malicious software. By fostering a culture of security awareness within the organization, IT departments can significantly reduce the risk of breaches caused by human error.

Overall, understanding the basics of network security is essential for corporate IT departments to effectively defend against cyber threats. By implementing a defense in depth strategy, conducting regular security assessments, and educating employees on best practices, organizations can strengthen their network defenses and protect sensitive data from malicious actors. By investing in cyber security training and incident response training, IT departments can stay ahead of the evolving threat landscape and safeguard their digital assets.

Common Network Security Threats

In today's digital age, businesses face numerous network security threats that can compromise sensitive information and disrupt operations. Understanding these threats is crucial for corporate IT departments, HR departments, cyber security professionals, and even hackers looking to stay ahead of potential attacks. This subchapter will explore some of the most common network security threats that organizations may encounter.

One of the most prevalent network security threats is malware, which includes viruses, worms, trojans, and ransomware. Malware can infect computers and networks, causing data breaches, financial losses, and system downtime. Corporate IT departments must implement strong anti-malware solutions and educate employees on safe internet practices to mitigate this threat.

Phishing attacks are another common network security threat that targets individuals through deceptive emails, messages, or websites. These attacks aim to trick recipients into revealing sensitive information such as passwords or financial details. HR departments should provide employees with regular training on how to recognize and report phishing attempts to protect the organization from potential data breaches.

Denial of Service (DoS) attacks can disrupt network services by overwhelming servers with a high volume of traffic, rendering them inaccessible to legitimate users. Cyber security professionals should implement robust DoS protection measures to mitigate the impact of these attacks and ensure business continuity. Incident response training is essential for quickly identifying and mitigating the effects of a DoS attack.

Insider threats pose a significant risk to network security, as employees with access to sensitive information may intentionally or unintentionally leak or misuse data. Security awareness training for employees can help prevent insider threats by educating staff on proper data handling procedures and the importance of confidentiality. Hackers may also take advantage of employees' lack of awareness to infiltrate networks, underscoring the need for continuous training and vigilance.

Lastly, insecure network configurations and outdated software can create vulnerabilities that hackers can exploit to gain unauthorized access to systems. Cyber security professionals should regularly conduct network security assessments to identify and address weaknesses in the organization's infrastructure.

By staying informed about common network security threats and implementing proactive security measures, businesses can better protect their digital assets and safeguard against potential cyber attacks.

Chapter 4: Cloud Security Training

Securing Cloud Infrastructure

In today's digital age, securing cloud infrastructure has become a top priority for organizations of all sizes. With the increasing reliance on cloud services for storing sensitive data and running critical applications, the need for robust security measures has never been greater. In this subchapter, we will explore the various threats facing cloud infrastructure and provide best practices for ensuring its protection.

One of the biggest challenges in securing cloud infrastructure is the shared responsibility model. While cloud service providers are responsible for securing the underlying infrastructure, organizations are still responsible for securing their data and applications. This means implementing strong access controls, encryption, and monitoring tools to detect and respond to potential threats.

When it comes to securing cloud infrastructure, a multi-layered approach is essential. This includes implementing firewalls, intrusion detection systems, and data loss prevention tools to protect against external threats. Additionally, organizations should conduct regular vulnerability assessments and penetration testing to identify and address any weaknesses in their cloud environment.

Another key aspect of securing cloud infrastructure is ensuring compliance with industry regulations and standards. With the increasing focus on data privacy and security, organizations must adhere to regulations such as GDPR and HIPAA to avoid costly fines and reputational damage. Implementing encryption, access controls, and audit trails can help organizations demonstrate compliance with these regulations.

In conclusion, securing cloud infrastructure is a critical task that requires a combination of technical expertise, robust security tools, and compliance with industry regulations. By following best practices such as implementing a multi-layered security approach, conducting regular assessments, and ensuring compliance with regulations, organizations can protect their cloud environment from cyber threats and safeguard their sensitive data. It is essential for corporate IT departments, HR departments, cyber security professionals, and even hackers to stay informed and trained in the latest techniques and tools for securing cloud infrastructure to effectively defend against cyber attacks.

Best Practices for Cloud Security

Cloud security is a critical aspect of cybersecurity for any organization that relies on cloud services to store, process, and manage sensitive data. In today's digital age, the threat landscape is constantly evolving, and organizations must stay vigilant to protect their data from malicious actors. In this subchapter, we will discuss best practices for cloud security that can help corporate IT departments, HR departments, cyber security professionals, and even hackers to enhance their cyber security posture.

One of the key best practices for cloud security is to ensure that data stored in the cloud is encrypted both in transit and at rest. Encryption helps protect data from unauthorized access and ensures that even if the data is intercepted, it cannot be read without the encryption key. Organizations should also implement strong access controls and authentication mechanisms to ensure that only authorized users can access sensitive data stored in the cloud.

Another best practice for cloud security is to regularly monitor and audit cloud services to detect any unauthorized access or suspicious activity. By implementing intrusion detection and prevention systems, organizations can quickly identify and respond to security incidents in the cloud. Additionally, organizations should regularly backup their data stored in the cloud to prevent data loss in the event of a security breach or ransomware attack.

Training employees on the importance of cloud security is also essential for enhancing an organization's cyber security posture. By providing cyber security training to employees, organizations can help them recognize phishing emails, social engineering attacks, and other common tactics used by cyber criminals. Security awareness training can empower employees to take proactive steps to protect sensitive data stored in the cloud and prevent security incidents.

Lastly, organizations should consider implementing multi-factor authentication for cloud services to add an extra layer of security. Multi-factor authentication requires users to provide two or more forms of verification before accessing sensitive data stored in the cloud. By implementing multi-factor authentication, organizations can significantly reduce the risk of unauthorized access and data breaches in the cloud. Overall, implementing these best practices for cloud security can help organizations strengthen their cyber security defenses and protect their data from cyber threats.

Chapter 5: Mobile Security Training

Mobile Device Security

Mobile devices have become an integral part of our daily lives, both at home and in the workplace. With the increasing reliance on mobile technology, it is crucial for corporate IT departments to prioritize mobile device security to protect sensitive information and prevent cyber attacks. This subchapter will delve into the importance of mobile device security, common threats faced by mobile users, best practices for securing mobile devices, and incident response strategies for handling security breaches.

One of the key reasons why mobile device security is essential is the sheer volume of sensitive information stored on these devices. From emails and contact information to financial data and proprietary business documents, mobile devices often contain a treasure trove of valuable data that can be targeted by cyber criminals. Without proper security measures in place, this information is at risk of being compromised, leading to financial loss, reputational damage, and regulatory penalties.

Mobile users face a variety of threats that can compromise the security of their devices and data. These threats include malware, phishing attacks, device theft, and unauthorized access to sensitive information. Hackers are constantly evolving their tactics to exploit vulnerabilities in mobile operating systems and applications, making it imperative for IT departments to stay ahead of the curve in terms of mobile security.

To mitigate the risks associated with mobile device security, IT departments should implement best practices such as enabling encryption, setting strong passwords, regularly updating software and applications, and using mobile device management (MDM) solutions. By taking a proactive approach to securing mobile devices, organizations can reduce the likelihood of a successful cyber attack and protect their sensitive information from unauthorized access.

In the event of a security breach involving a mobile device, it is crucial for organizations to have an incident response plan in place to contain the threat, investigate the incident, and remediate any damage. This plan should outline the roles and responsibilities of key stakeholders, establish communication protocols, and detail the steps to be taken to restore the security of the affected device and prevent similar incidents in the future. By being prepared to respond effectively to security breaches, organizations can minimize the impact of cyber attacks and safeguard their critical assets.

Mobile App Security

Mobile app security is a critical aspect of overall cybersecurity, especially in today's digital world where mobile devices are an integral part of our daily lives. As more and more companies rely on mobile apps to conduct business, it is essential for corporate IT departments to prioritize mobile app security to protect sensitive data and prevent cyber attacks.

One of the key challenges in mobile app security is the sheer number of vulnerabilities that can be exploited by hackers. From insecure data storage to inadequate encryption protocols, mobile apps are often targeted by cyber criminals looking to gain unauthorized access to sensitive information. Corporate IT departments must conduct regular security assessments and penetration testing to identify and address these vulnerabilities before they can be exploited.

HR departments also play a crucial role in mobile app security by ensuring that employees are trained on best practices for using mobile apps securely. This includes educating employees on the risks of downloading apps from untrusted sources, using strong passwords, and being vigilant for phishing attacks that may target mobile devices. By promoting a culture of security awareness, HR departments can help prevent data breaches and protect the company's reputation.

Cyber security professionals and hackers alike can benefit from specialized training in mobile app security to stay ahead of the latest threats and vulnerabilities. Courses on mobile security training cover topics such as secure coding practices, mobile device management, and secure authentication methods.

By investing in ongoing training and certification programs, cyber security professionals can enhance their skills and expertise in mobile app security, ultimately strengthening the overall cybersecurity posture of the organization.

In conclusion, mobile app security is a critical component of a comprehensive cybersecurity strategy for corporate IT departments.

By prioritizing mobile security training, conducting regular security assessments, and promoting security awareness among employees, companies can mitigate the risks of data breaches and cyber attacks. Whether you are a cyber security professional, hacker, or IT department looking to enhance your mobile app security defenses, investing in training and education is essential to protecting sensitive data and safeguarding against evolving cyber threats.

Chapter 6: Web Application Security Training

Common Web Application Vulnerabilities

In today's digital age, web applications have become an integral part of corporate IT departments. However, with the rise of cyber threats, it is crucial for organizations to be aware of common web application vulnerabilities that can compromise their data security. This subchapter will explore some of the most prevalent vulnerabilities that IT departments need to be vigilant about in order to defend their digital realm.

One of the most common web application vulnerabilities is SQL injection, where attackers can insert malicious SQL code into input fields to access and manipulate sensitive data stored in the database. This can lead to data breaches and compromise the confidentiality of critical information. To prevent SQL injection attacks, organizations should implement input validation and parameterized queries to sanitize user input and prevent unauthorized access to the database.

Another common vulnerability is cross-site scripting (XSS), where attackers inject malicious scripts into web pages viewed by other users. This can lead to the theft of sensitive information such as login credentials and financial data. To mitigate XSS attacks, organizations should implement proper input validation and output encoding to prevent malicious scripts from executing on web pages and compromising user data.

Insecure deserialization is another prevalent web application vulnerability where attackers can manipulate serialized objects to execute arbitrary code on the server. This can lead to remote code execution and compromise the integrity of the web application. To prevent insecure deserialization attacks, organizations should validate and sanitize serialized objects before deserializing them to prevent malicious code execution.

Security misconfigurations are also a common web application vulnerability where organizations fail to properly configure security settings, leaving their web applications vulnerable to attacks. This can include default credentials, unnecessary services, and outdated software that can be exploited by attackers. To mitigate security misconfigurations, organizations should regularly audit and update their security settings to ensure that their web applications are properly secured against potential threats.

Lastly, insufficient logging and monitoring is a common web application vulnerability where organizations fail to log and monitor security events, making it difficult to detect and respond to security incidents in a timely manner. This can lead to delayed incident response and increased damage to the organization's reputation and bottom line. To improve logging and monitoring, organizations should implement robust logging mechanisms and security information and event management (SIEM) solutions to track and analyze security events in real-time and respond to incidents promptly. By being aware of these common web application vulnerabilities and implementing best practices to mitigate them, organizations can defend their digital realm and safeguard their sensitive data from cyber threats.

Secure Coding Practices

In the world of cybersecurity, secure coding practices are essential for protecting sensitive data and preventing cyber attacks. This subchapter will cover some best practices that corporate IT departments, HR departments, cybersecurity professionals, and even hackers should follow to ensure the security of their systems.

One important secure coding practice is input validation. This involves checking user input to ensure that it is within acceptable parameters before processing it. By validating input, developers can prevent common vulnerabilities such as SQL injection and cross-site scripting attacks. This practice is crucial for protecting web applications, mobile apps, and other software from malicious actors.

Another key aspect of secure coding is proper error handling. When errors occur in a system, they can provide valuable information to attackers. By implementing robust error handling mechanisms, developers can prevent attackers from exploiting vulnerabilities and gaining unauthorized access to sensitive data. This practice is especially important for incident response training, as it can help organizations quickly identify and address security incidents.

Secure coding practices also extend to network security. By implementing encryption protocols such as SSL/TLS, organizations can protect data in transit from eavesdroppers. Additionally, secure coding practices for cloud security training involve properly configuring cloud services and implementing access controls to prevent unauthorized access to cloud resources.

In the realm of industrial control system security training, secure coding practices are essential for protecting critical infrastructure from cyber attacks. By following best practices such as secure coding guidelines and regular code reviews, organizations can prevent attackers from exploiting vulnerabilities in industrial systems. This practice is crucial for maintaining the integrity and availability of critical infrastructure.

Overall, secure coding practices are essential for protecting corporate IT systems from cyber threats. By following best practices such as input validation, error handling, network security, and industrial control system security training, organizations can reduce the risk of data breaches and cyber attacks. It is important for cybersecurity professionals, hackers, and employees to stay up to date on the latest secure coding practices to ensure the security of their systems.

Chapter 7: Industrial Control System Security Training

Understanding Industrial Control Systems

Industrial control systems (ICS) are critical components in the operation of many industries, including manufacturing, energy, and transportation. These systems are responsible for controlling and monitoring physical processes, such as machinery, equipment, and infrastructure. Understanding how these systems work is essential for ensuring the security and reliability of industrial operations.

One key aspect of industrial control systems is their reliance on interconnected networks and software applications. These systems are often connected to the internet or other external networks, making them vulnerable to cyber attacks. Corporate IT departments must be aware of the potential risks associated with these systems and take steps to protect them from malicious actors.

In addition to understanding the technical aspects of industrial control systems, it is also important to consider the human element. HR departments play a crucial role in ensuring that employees are trained in cybersecurity best practices and are aware of the risks associated with industrial control systems. By providing ongoing training and education, HR departments can help prevent security breaches and protect critical infrastructure.

For cyber security professionals and hackers alike, understanding industrial control systems is essential for identifying vulnerabilities and developing effective defense strategies. Incident response training is particularly important in this context, as it allows organizations to quickly detect and respond to security incidents before they escalate. By staying informed about the latest threats and vulnerabilities, cyber security professionals can help protect industrial control systems from cyber attacks.

Overall, industrial control system security training is a crucial component of any comprehensive cyber security program. By educating employees, IT departments, and cyber security professionals about the unique challenges and risks associated with these systems, organizations can better protect themselves from cyber threats. With the right training and tools in place, businesses can ensure the security and reliability of their industrial operations in an increasingly digital world.

Securing Industrial Control Systems

Industrial Control Systems (ICS) are the backbone of many critical infrastructure sectors such as energy, water, transportation, and manufacturing. These systems are increasingly becoming targets for cyber attacks, as hackers seek to disrupt operations, steal sensitive data, or cause physical damage. In order to protect these vital systems from cyber threats, it is essential for organizations to implement robust security measures.

One of the key steps in securing Industrial Control Systems is to conduct a thorough risk assessment. This involves identifying potential vulnerabilities in the system, assessing the likelihood and impact of different cyber threats, and prioritizing security measures accordingly. By understanding the specific risks facing their ICS, organizations can develop a targeted security strategy that effectively mitigates potential threats.

In addition to conducting risk assessments, organizations should also implement strong access controls to prevent unauthorized individuals from gaining access to their Industrial Control Systems. This includes using multi-factor authentication, restricting access to sensitive systems and data, and regularly monitoring user activity for any signs of suspicious behavior. By limiting access to only authorized personnel, organizations can reduce the risk of insider threats and external cyber attacks.

Another important aspect of securing Industrial Control Systems is to regularly update and patch system software and firmware. Many cyber attacks exploit known vulnerabilities in outdated software, so organizations must stay vigilant in keeping their systems up to date with the latest security patches. By regularly monitoring for new vulnerabilities and proactively patching them, organizations can reduce their exposure to cyber threats and improve the overall security of their Industrial Control Systems.

Finally, organizations should also consider implementing network segmentation to isolate their Industrial Control Systems from other parts of their network. By creating separate network segments for their ICS, organizations can limit the potential impact of a cyber attack and prevent attackers from moving laterally within their network. This additional layer of protection can help organizations contain and mitigate the effects of a cyber attack, reducing the potential damage to their critical infrastructure and operations.

Chapter 8: Cyber Threat Intelligence Training

Introduction to Cyber Threat Intelligence

In today's digital age, the threat landscape is constantly evolving, and organizations must be proactive in defending their digital assets against cyber attacks. This is where Cyber Threat Intelligence comes into play. Cyber Threat Intelligence is the process of collecting, analyzing, and disseminating information about potential cyber threats to help organizations understand and mitigate their risks.

For Corporate IT departments, having a solid understanding of Cyber Threat Intelligence is essential for identifying and responding to cyber threats in a timely manner. By analyzing indicators of compromise, such as IP addresses, domain names, and malware signatures, IT departments can proactively defend against potential attacks before they cause significant damage.

The HR department also plays a crucial role in Cyber Threat Intelligence by ensuring that employees are trained on how to recognize and respond to potential threats. By providing security awareness training for employees, HR departments can help create a culture of cybersecurity within the organization, where everyone is vigilant and proactive in protecting sensitive information.

For Cyber Security professionals, understanding Cyber Threat Intelligence is a key component of their job. By monitoring and analyzing threat intelligence feeds, security professionals can stay ahead of emerging threats and take proactive measures to protect their organization's network and data.

Even hackers can benefit from understanding Cyber Threat Intelligence, as it can help them identify vulnerabilities and weaknesses in their own systems and networks. By learning how cyber threats are identified and mitigated, hackers can improve their own security practices and reduce their risk of being targeted by malicious actors.

Overall, Cyber Threat Intelligence is a crucial component of any organization's cybersecurity strategy. By staying informed about potential threats and taking proactive measures to defend against them, organizations can reduce their risk of falling victim to cyber attacks and protect their valuable digital assets.

Utilizing Threat Intelligence for Defense

Utilizing threat intelligence for defense is a crucial aspect of protecting your organization from cyber threats. Threat intelligence involves gathering, analyzing, and understanding information about potential cyber threats in order to proactively defend against them. In today's digital age, where cyber attacks are becoming increasingly sophisticated and frequent, having a strong threat intelligence program in place is essential for the security of your organization.

Corporate IT departments play a key role in implementing and managing threat intelligence programs within their organizations. By staying informed about the latest cyber threats and vulnerabilities, IT teams can better protect their networks and systems from potential attacks. HR departments also play a role in threat intelligence by ensuring that employees are trained on how to recognize and respond to potential threats, such as phishing emails or social engineering attacks.

Cyber security professionals are tasked with analyzing threat intelligence data to identify patterns and trends that could indicate a potential cyber attack. By monitoring and analyzing this information, security professionals can develop strategies to defend against potential threats and mitigate any potential risks to the organization. Hackers can also benefit from threat intelligence by understanding the latest tactics and techniques used by cyber criminals, allowing them to better protect their own systems and networks from attack.

Training in cyber threat intelligence is essential for IT departments, HR departments, cyber security professionals, and hackers alike. By understanding how to gather and analyze threat intelligence data, individuals can better protect their organizations and themselves from potential cyber threats. Whether it's incident response training, network security training, or security awareness training for employees, having a strong foundation in threat intelligence is key to defending against cyber attacks in today's digital landscape. By investing in cyber threat intelligence training, organizations can stay one step ahead of cyber criminals and protect their valuable data and assets from harm.

Chapter 9: Security Awareness Training for Employees

Importance of Security Awareness

In today's digital age, the importance of security awareness cannot be emphasized enough. With cyber threats becoming more sophisticated and prevalent, it is crucial for individuals and organizations to be vigilant and proactive in protecting their sensitive information. This subchapter will delve into the significance of security awareness and how it plays a vital role in defending the digital realm.

For Corporate IT departments, security awareness training is essential in ensuring that employees are equipped with the knowledge and skills to identify and respond to potential security threats. By educating staff on best practices for data protection, password management, and phishing awareness, organizations can significantly reduce the risk of a cyber attack. Additionally, regular training sessions can help reinforce the importance of security protocols and instill a culture of security consciousness within the company.

The HR department also plays a crucial role in promoting security awareness within an organization. By collaborating with IT professionals to develop comprehensive training programs, HR can help ensure that employees are well-informed about cyber threats and know how to safeguard company data. Furthermore, HR can incorporate security awareness into the onboarding process for new hires, setting a strong foundation for a security-conscious workplace environment.

For Cyber Security professionals, staying up-to-date on the latest security trends and threats is vital for effectively defending against cyber attacks. By continuously enhancing their skills through incident response training, network security training, cloud security training, and other specialized courses, professionals can better protect their organization's digital assets. Additionally, cyber threat intelligence training can provide valuable insights into emerging threats and help security teams proactively mitigate risks.

Even for Hackers, understanding the importance of security awareness is crucial in ethical hacking practices. By recognizing the impact of cyber attacks on individuals and organizations, hackers can leverage their skills for positive purposes, such as identifying vulnerabilities and helping to strengthen security measures. By participating in security awareness training for employees, hackers can contribute to a safer digital environment for all users.

In conclusion, security awareness is a fundamental aspect of cyber security training that benefits all stakeholders in the digital realm. By prioritizing security education and fostering a culture of vigilance, organizations can effectively defend against cyber threats and safeguard their sensitive information. Whether you are a Corporate IT department, HR department, Cyber Security professional, or Hacker, investing in security awareness training is key to staying one step ahead of cyber criminals and protecting the integrity of digital assets.

Developing an Effective Security Awareness Program

Developing an effective security awareness program is crucial for organizations to protect their digital assets and prevent cyber attacks. This subchapter will provide insights and guidance for corporate IT departments, HR departments, cyber security professionals, and even hackers on how to create and implement a successful security awareness program.

The first step in developing a security awareness program is to assess the current level of awareness within the organization. This can be done through surveys, interviews, or even simulated phishing attacks to gauge employees' knowledge and understanding of security best practices. By identifying areas of weakness, organizations can tailor their training programs to address specific needs and vulnerabilities.

Next, organizations should establish clear objectives and goals for their security awareness program. These may include reducing the number of security incidents, increasing employee compliance with security policies, or improving incident response times. By setting measurable goals, organizations can track the effectiveness of their training efforts and make adjustments as needed.

Once objectives are established, organizations should develop a comprehensive training curriculum that covers a wide range of security topics, including network security, cloud security, mobile security, and web application security. Training should be tailored to employees' specific roles and responsibilities within the organization, ensuring that each individual receives the information they need to protect sensitive data and prevent cyber attacks.

In addition to formal training sessions, organizations should also consider incorporating gamification and interactive elements into their security awareness program. This can help engage employees and make learning about security best practices more enjoyable and memorable. By making security training a fun and interactive experience, organizations can increase employee participation and retention of important security concepts.

Finally, organizations should regularly evaluate the effectiveness of their security awareness program through metrics such as employee participation rates, incident response times, and security incident trends.

By continuously monitoring and adjusting their training efforts, organizations can ensure that their employees are well-equipped to defend against cyber threats and protect the digital realm.

Chapter 10: Advanced Cyber Security Techniques

Penetration Testing

Penetration testing, also known as ethical hacking, is a crucial component of any comprehensive cybersecurity strategy. This practice involves simulating real-world cyberattacks on an organization's systems, networks, and applications to identify vulnerabilities that could be exploited by malicious actors. By conducting penetration tests, IT departments can proactively identify and address weaknesses in their security posture before they are exploited by cybercriminals.

One of the key benefits of penetration testing is that it provides valuable insights into an organization's security defenses. By mimicking the tactics and techniques used by hackers, penetration testers can uncover vulnerabilities that may have otherwise gone undetected. This information allows IT departments to prioritize their remediation efforts and strengthen their overall security posture.

For HR departments, penetration testing can also be a valuable tool for assessing the security awareness and readiness of employees. By conducting simulated phishing attacks and social engineering tests, organizations can identify gaps in their employees' security knowledge and behavior. This information can then be used to tailor security awareness training programs to address these weaknesses and reduce the risk of successful cyberattacks.

Cybersecurity professionals and hackers alike can benefit from penetration testing training. For professionals in the cybersecurity field, penetration testing provides valuable hands-on experience in identifying and exploiting vulnerabilities. This practical knowledge can enhance their incident response capabilities and make them more effective at defending against cyber threats. For hackers, penetration testing training can provide a legal and ethical outlet for their skills, allowing them to use their expertise to help organizations improve their security defenses.

In conclusion, penetration testing is a critical practice for organizations looking to strengthen their cybersecurity defenses. By simulating real-world cyberattacks, IT departments can identify and address vulnerabilities before they are exploited by malicious actors. HR departments can use penetration testing to assess the security awareness of employees and tailor training programs accordingly. Cybersecurity professionals and hackers can also benefit from penetration testing training, gaining valuable hands-on experience that can enhance their incident response capabilities.

Incident Response Simulation Exercises

In the world of cybersecurity, being prepared for potential incidents is crucial. Incident response simulation exercises are an effective way for organizations to test their readiness and response capabilities in the event of a cyber attack. These exercises involve creating realistic scenarios that mimic real-world threats, allowing teams to practice how they would react and mitigate the impact of an attack.

One of the key benefits of conducting incident response simulation exercises is that they help organizations identify weaknesses in their security posture. By simulating different types of cyber attacks, teams can uncover vulnerabilities in their systems, processes, and protocols that may have otherwise gone unnoticed. This information can then be used to strengthen the organization's defenses and improve overall cybersecurity readiness.

Furthermore, incident response simulation exercises provide valuable training opportunities for IT and cybersecurity professionals. These exercises allow team members to practice their roles and responsibilities in a controlled environment, helping them develop the skills and knowledge needed to effectively respond to real-world threats. Through hands-on experience, participants can hone their incident response skills and improve their ability to work together as a cohesive unit during a crisis.

For hackers, participating in incident response simulation exercises can offer a unique perspective on how organizations defend against cyber attacks. By simulating different attack scenarios, hackers can gain insight into the strategies and tactics used by defenders, allowing them to better understand the defensive measures in place and potentially identify new ways to exploit vulnerabilities. This knowledge can be invaluable for hackers looking to improve their own skills and stay ahead of the curve in the ever-evolving world of cybersecurity.

Overall, incident response simulation exercises play a crucial role in helping organizations prepare for and respond to cyber threats. By creating realistic scenarios, identifying weaknesses, and providing valuable training opportunities, these exercises are an essential component of any comprehensive cybersecurity training program. Whether you are a member of a corporate IT department, HR department, cybersecurity professional, or even a hacker, participating in these exercises can help you sharpen your skills, enhance your knowledge, and better protect your organization from cyber attacks.

Chapter 11: Ethical Hacking Training

Introduction to Ethical Hacking

Ethical hacking, also known as penetration testing or white-hat hacking, is the practice of testing computer systems, networks, and applications for security vulnerabilities in a controlled manner. Unlike malicious hackers, ethical hackers use their skills to identify and fix weaknesses in a company's digital infrastructure before they can be exploited by cybercriminals. This proactive approach to cybersecurity is crucial in today's rapidly evolving threat landscape, where cyber attacks are becoming more frequent and sophisticated.

For corporate IT departments, ethical hacking plays a vital role in assessing the security posture of their organization and identifying potential weaknesses that could be exploited by malicious actors. By conducting regular penetration tests and vulnerability assessments, IT teams can stay one step ahead of cyber threats and prevent costly data breaches. Ethical hacking is an essential component of a comprehensive cybersecurity strategy, helping companies safeguard their sensitive information and protect their reputation.

HR departments can benefit from understanding the basics of ethical hacking as well, as they play a key role in hiring and training cybersecurity professionals. By familiarizing themselves with the principles of ethical hacking, HR professionals can better assess the skills and qualifications of job candidates and ensure that their organization has the right talent in place to defend against cyber threats. Additionally, HR departments can use ethical hacking training as a tool for professional development, helping employees stay up-to-date on the latest cybersecurity techniques and best practices.

Cyber security professionals and hackers alike can benefit from delving into the world of ethical hacking. For cyber security professionals, ethical hacking provides valuable insights into the mindset and techniques of malicious hackers, enabling them to better defend against cyber attacks and respond effectively to security incidents. By gaining hands-on experience with ethical hacking tools and methodologies, security professionals can enhance their skills and advance their careers in the field of cybersecurity.

Overall, ethical hacking is a valuable skill set for anyone involved in cybersecurity training, incident response training, network security training, cloud security training, mobile security training, web application security training, industrial control system security training, cyber threat intelligence training, or security awareness training for employees. By understanding the principles of ethical hacking and incorporating them into their training programs, organizations can better prepare their employees to defend against cyber threats and protect their digital assets. Ethical hacking is not just a technical skill – it is a mindset that emphasizes proactive risk management and continuous improvement in cybersecurity practices.

Hands-on Hacking Exercises

In this subchapter, we will delve into the importance of hands-on hacking exercises as part of cyber security training for corporate IT departments. These exercises are crucial in preparing IT professionals to defend against real-world cyber threats and attacks. By immersing themselves in simulated hacking scenarios, participants can gain valuable experience and insights into the tactics and techniques used by malicious actors.

Hands-on hacking exercises provide a practical and interactive learning environment for IT professionals to test their skills and knowledge in a controlled setting. These exercises can range from basic penetration testing to more advanced red team vs. blue team simulations. By actively engaging in these exercises, participants can better understand the vulnerabilities in their organization's systems and networks, as well as develop the necessary skills to identify and mitigate these vulnerabilities.

For HR departments, hands-on hacking exercises can also be valuable in assessing the proficiency and readiness of IT professionals in defending against cyber threats. By incorporating these exercises into training programs, HR departments can ensure that their IT teams are well-equipped to handle potential security incidents and breaches. Additionally, these exercises can help identify areas for improvement and further training for IT professionals.

Cyber security professionals and hackers alike can benefit from hands-on hacking exercises by honing their skills and staying up-to-date on the latest trends and tactics in cyber security.

These exercises provide a platform for continuous learning and professional development, allowing participants to push themselves beyond their comfort zones and expand their knowledge of cyber security. By actively engaging in these exercises, cyber security professionals can enhance their expertise and become more effective in defending against cyber threats.

Overall, hands-on hacking exercises are a critical component of cyber security training for corporate IT departments. By providing a practical and immersive learning experience, these exercises can help IT professionals develop the skills and knowledge needed to defend against cyber threats effectively. Whether you are looking to enhance your incident response training, network security training, or cloud security training, hands-on hacking exercises can provide valuable insights and experiences that will benefit your organization in the long run.

Chapter 12: Conclusion and Next Steps

Recap of Key Concepts

In this subchapter, we will recap some of the key concepts discussed throughout this book, "Defending the Digital Realm: A Cyber

Security Training Guide for Corporate IT Departments." These concepts are essential for all members of the Corporate IT department, HR Department, Cyber Security professionals, and even hackers to understand in order to effectively defend against cyber threats.

First and foremost, it is crucial to understand the importance of continuous cyber security training. Cyber threats are constantly evolving, and it is essential for IT professionals to stay up-to-date on the latest trends and techniques used by hackers. By investing in ongoing training, organizations can better protect their networks and data from potential breaches.

Another key concept to remember is the importance of incident response training. In the event of a cyber attack, it is essential for IT professionals to know how to quickly and effectively respond to the threat. This includes identifying the source of the attack, containing the breach, and restoring systems to normal operation as soon as possible.

Network security training is also vital in today's digital age. With the increasing number of devices connected to corporate networks, it is essential for IT professionals to understand how to secure these networks from potential threats. This includes implementing firewalls, intrusion detection systems, and other security measures to protect sensitive data.

Cloud security training is another important concept to consider. As more organizations move their data and applications to the cloud, it is essential for IT professionals to understand how to secure these environments from potential attacks. This includes implementing strong authentication measures, encryption, and other security controls to protect data in the cloud.

Finally, it is crucial for organizations to invest in security awareness training for employees. Human error is one of the leading causes of data breaches, so it is essential for employees to understand the importance of cyber security and how to protect themselves and their organization from potential threats. By providing ongoing training and education, organizations can better defend against cyber threats and keep their data secure.

Continuing Education Opportunities

In the fast-paced world of cyber security, staying ahead of the curve is crucial to effectively defend against digital threats. For corporate IT departments, HR departments, cyber security professionals, and even hackers looking to expand their knowledge and skills, continuing education opportunities are essential. Whether it's cyber security training, incident response training, network security training, cloud security training, mobile security training, web application security training, industrial control system security training, cyber threat intelligence training, or security awareness training for employees, there are a variety of options available to help individuals and organizations stay up-to-date on the latest trends and best practices in the field.

One of the most popular continuing education opportunities for cyber security professionals is cyber security training. This type of training covers a wide range of topics, including cryptography, network security, ethical hacking, and more. Many organizations offer online courses, workshops, and certifications that can help professionals improve their skills and advance their careers in the field. Additionally, attending industry conferences and seminars can provide valuable networking opportunities and insight into emerging trends and technologies.

Incident response training is another important area of continuing education for cyber security professionals. This type of training focuses on preparing individuals and organizations to effectively respond to and recover from cyber security incidents, such as data breaches or malware attacks. By practicing simulated scenarios and learning best practices for incident response, professionals can better protect their organizations and minimize the impact of potential security incidents.

Network security training is essential for IT departments and cyber security professionals responsible for protecting their organization's networks from cyber threats. This type of training covers topics such as firewalls, intrusion detection systems, and secure network design. By understanding the latest threats and vulnerabilities facing networks, professionals can implement effective security measures to defend against potential attacks.

Cloud security training is also becoming increasingly important as more organizations transition to cloud-based services. This type of training helps professionals understand the unique security challenges associated with cloud computing and develop strategies to secure data and applications in the cloud. By staying informed on the latest cloud security best practices and technologies, professionals can ensure the confidentiality, integrity, and availability of their organization's cloud-based resources.

Overall, continuing education opportunities in cyber security are essential for individuals and organizations looking to stay ahead of the ever-evolving digital landscape. By investing in training and development programs, professionals can enhance their skills, expand their knowledge, and better protect their organizations from cyber threats. Whether it's cyber security training, incident response training, network security training, or another specialty area, there are plenty of opportunities available to help individuals and organizations succeed in the field of cyber security.

www.ingramcontent.com/pod-product-compliance
Lightning Source LLC
Chambersburg PA
CBHW070420230526
45471CB00006B/2898